THE

ACT OF INCORPORATION

AND THE

BY-LAWS

OF THE

Massachusetts Homoeopathic Medical Society.

BOSTON:
PRINTED BY FRED ROGERS,
159 WASHINGTON STREET.
1864.

ACT OF INCORPORATION.

Commonwealth of Massachusetts.

IN THE YEAR ONE THOUSAND EIGHT HUNDRED AND FIFTY-SIX.

AN ACT TO INCORPORATE THE MASSACHUSETTS HOMŒOPATHIC MEDICAL SOCIETY.

Be it enacted by the Senate and House of Representatives in General Court assembled, and by the authority of the same, as follows:—

Sect. 1.—Samuel Gregg, William Wesselhoeft, Luther Clark, George Russell, Milton Fuller, John A. Tarbell, David Thayer, their associates and successors, physicians, be, and they hereby are, made a Corporation, by the name of the Massachusetts Homœopathic Medical Society, with all the powers and privileges, and subject to all the duties, liabilities, and restrictions, set forth in the forty-fourth chapter of the Revised Statutes.

Sect. 2.—Said Corporation may hold real and personal estate to the amount of fifty thousand dollars.

Sect. 3.—The members of said Society shall not be liable to be mustered or enrolled in the militia of this Commonwealth.

Sect. 4.—The members of said Society, or such of their officers or members as they shall appoint, shall have full power and authority to examine all candidates for membership, concerning the practice of specific medicine and surgery, provided said candidates shall sustain a good moral character, and shall present letters testimonial of their qualifications from some legally authorized medical institution; and if, upon such examination, the said candidates shall be found qualified for membership, they shall receive the approbation of the Society.

Sect. 5.—This act shall take effect from and after its passage.

House of Representatives, May 30, 1856.

Passed to be enacted, CHARLES A. PHELPS, *Speaker*.

In Senate, May 31, 1856.

Passed to be enacted, ELIHU C. BAKER, *President*.

June 3, 1856. Approved, HENRY J. GARDNER.

Secretary's Office, Boston, June 24, 1856.

A true copy.

Attest: FRANCIS DE WITT,
Secretary of the Commonwealth.

BY-LAWS

OF THE

Massachusetts Homoeopathic Medical Society,

REVISED AND ADOPTED APRIL 13TH, 1864.

SOCIETY.

I. THIS Society shall consist of the persons named in the Act of Incorporation, and such other persons as may have been elected members in accordance with its By-laws.

OFFICERS OF THE SOCIETY.

II. The Society, at its Annual Meeting, shall elect, by ballot, a President, two Vice-Presidents, Corresponding Secretary, Recording Secretary, Treasurer, Librarian, and five Censors, who shall together constitute an Executive Committee, to whom shall be intrusted the general business of the Society when it is not in session; the appointment of all standing committees, and such other committees as they may deem expedient; and the selection of some suitable person to deliver an address, at the annual meeting of the Society, on some subject connected with medical science. At every annual meeting, they shall present a report of their proceedings during the past year; and shall also furnish a list of two candidates for each office of the Society for the ensuing year. The officers shall continue in office till the adjournment of the annual meeting next after their election, at which time the duties of the newly elected officers shall commence.

DUTIES OF THE OFFICERS.

III. The *President* shall preside at all meetings of the Society and of the Executive Committee; and shall deliver an address before the Society, at the commencement of the annual meeting.

In case of the absence or other disability of the President, his duties shall devolve on the Vice-President, by seniority, if present; otherwise on such person as the meeting may appoint.

Members shall not be eligible to the office of President more than once in five years.

IV. The *Corresponding Secretary* shall have the charge and custody of all letters and communications transmitted to the Society; and to him they should be addressed. He shall prepare and transmit whatever communications the Society or Executive Committee may direct; and he shall perform such other duties as may be assigned to him.

V. The *Recording Secretary* shall give notice and keep a record of all the meetings of the Society and of the Executive Committee. He shall append to the notices of the annual and semi-annual meeting, the names of those candidates for membership that have been reported to the Executive Committee. He shall have charge of all papers and communications belonging to the Society; and shall read, at the meetings of the Society, all such communications as the Executive Committee may direct. He shall notify the chairman of every committee appointed by the Society or Executive Committee, of his appointment, in each case stating the commission and the names of the committee. On or before the first of April, annually, he shall transmit to the Treasurer a list of all who have become members of the Society during the year.

VI. The *Treasurer* shall solicit and receive all money due to the Society, together with all bequests and donations; and shall pay all bills after they shall have been approved by the Executive Committee, which approval shall be certified to by the Recording Secretary. He shall keep an accurate account of all receipts and expenditures, and shall give such bonds for the faithful performance of his duties as the Society may require. He shall submit his accounts to such examination as the Executive Committee may direct; and shall annually make a statement of his doings, and of the state of the funds in his hands, to the Society.

VII. The *Librarian* shall have in his custody and charge all the books and apparatus of the Society. He shall keep an accurate register of the same, and arrange them in a proper manner; and shall make such disposition of them, from time to time, as the Executive Committee may direct for the benefit of the members. He shall receive and record all donations made in his department to the Society, and shall make a report at the annual meeting.

VIII. The *Censors* shall examine the qualifications of all persons presenting themselves for membership, and for that purpose shall hold meetings on the days of the annual and semi-annual meetings, and at such other times as they may deem necessary. They shall report the names of all approved candidates for membership to the Executive Committee at least three months before their election as members by the Society.

IX. There shall be a *Committee on the Materia Medica*, who shall select medicines for proving; and shall, at the expense of the Society, obtain and distribute the same to its members, or such other persons as they may deem suitable. They shall receive and examine communications upon the *materia medica* from the members of the Society, and report thereon at any regular meeting.

X. There shall be a *Committee on Clinical Medicine*, who shall receive and examine communications proper to this department, and report thereon at any regular meeting. They shall also report upon any epidemics which may have occurred in the state or country during the year,—their characteristics, mode of treatment, and results; and such other facts relating to the practice of medicine as they may deem important.

XI. There shall be a *Committee of Publication* consisting of the President, Recording Secretary, and at least three other members, to whom all matter for Publication shall be referred, and under whose direction it shall be issued; the expense of which shall not exceed in any year a sum designated by the Executive Committee.

XII. There shall be a *Committee of Arrangements* whose duty shall be to make such arrangements as will add to the interest and importance of the annual and semi-annual meetings, such as selecting a suitable place for the meetings, soliciting communications, appointing subjects for discussion, providing refreshments for members, &c., subject to the direction of the Executive Committee.

XIII. There shall be a *Committee on the Library*, who shall select and obtain such books and publications as they may be able to, by donation, subscription, or purchase with funds set apart for that purpose by the Executive Committee or Society.

XIV. The Executive and all other Committees shall have power to fill their own vacancies.

MEMBERSHIP.

XV. Any person who has received the degree of Doctor of Medicine from a legally authorized medical institution, who sustains a good moral character, and practices medicine in accordance with the maxim, "*Similia similibus curantur*," may become eligible to membership, after having been examined and approved by the Board of Censors. He shall be elected by ballot at the annual or semi-annual meeting, and, after his election, shall sign the By-laws before becoming a member.

HONORARY AND CORRESPONDING MEMBERS.

XVI. Persons who have excelled, or made any great advancement in medical or other science, may be elected honorary members, and physicians of eminence residing out of the State, may be elected corresponding members of the Society by a two-thirds vote of the members present at any stated meeting, provided the said person shall have been approved by the Executive Committee. Honorary and corresponding members shall be entitled to the diploma of the Society, and to participate in its proceedings in meetings devoted to scientific subjects.

XVII. Every member shall receive the diploma of the Society, signed by the President and Secretary, for which he shall, upon his election, pay the sum of five dollars.

XVIII. Any member in good standing shall have the privilege of withdrawing from the Society, by giving notice, in writing, of such intention, and paying all arrearages due to the Society.

RETIRED MEMBERS.

XIX. Members on removing from the State, or on retiring from practice, may, provided all their dues to the Society are paid, by vote of the Executive Committee, be placed on the list of retired members, and as such, shall be exempt from any assessments, and shall not receive, except by courtesy, any of the publications of the Society, nor be entitled to speak or vote at any of its meetings.

XX. Any person who has resigned his membership, or been placed on the list of retired members, may, on application in writing, be reinstated by vote of the Society at any regular meeting.

Any member removing out of the State shall have liberty to retain his membership, on paying his annual assessment.

XXI. Any member may be expelled from the Society, or, having resigned his membership, may be deprived of his privileges, by a vote of two-thirds of the members present at any regular meeting, upon charges of the following description; provided the charge or charges against him have first been considered by the Executive Committee, and provided he has been notified of the same by the Secretary, and an opportunity has thereby been given him to make his defence before the Society: —

1. For any gross and notorious immorality or infamous crime under the laws of the land.

2. For any attempt to subvert the objects or injure the reputation of the Society.

3. For advertising, publicly vending, or pretending to the knowledge and use of any secret nostrum.

4. For furnishing to any person, or presenting in his own behalf, a false certificate of character and studies as a student of

medicine, tending to deceive the public, or the Censors of the Society.

5. For habitually furnishing advice or holding professional consultations with persons who practice medicine without the necessary acquirements to entitle them to the respect, confidence or courtesy of the members of the Society.

XXII. As the object of the Society is to improve the science of medicine, to increase the influence and usefulness of its members, and to secure greater harmony and friendship among them, therefore it is of the highest importance that each member should so conduct himself, both in his private and professional life, as to command the entire respect of his colleagues.

Every person who becomes a member is understood to take upon himself an obligation to communicate to the Society any discoveries he shall have made relating to the science of medicine or surgery, and to co-operate in such measures as may be adopted by the Society for the advancement of these sciences; and, on his refusal to do so, he shall be subject to such censure as the Society, by a two-thirds vote, shall inflict.

XXIII. Every member of the Society shall be assessed annually three dollars ($3), and such other assessments as a majority of the members, at any legal meeting, may determine.

DELEGATES.

XXIV. The Executive Committee may appoint delegates to other Societies and Associations whenever they deem it advisable to do so; and such delegates shall receive certificates of appointment from the Recording Secretary.

Accredited delegates from other Societies and Associations shall be allowed to participate in the scientific deliberations of this Society.

MEETINGS OF THE SOCIETY.

XXV. The annual meeting of the Society shall be held on the second Wednesday of April, and the semi-annual meeting on the second Wednesday of October, at ten o'clock, A. M., in such one of the cities or towns of the Commonwealth as the Executive Committee may determine. A special meeting of the Society shall be called by the President, on the written request of ten members, stating the object of said meeting.

MEETINGS OF THE EXECUTIVE COMMITTEE.

XXVI. The *Executive Committee* shall meet on the third Wednesday of April, July, October, and January. At the first or annual meeting the Committees and the Orator shall be appointed for the ensuing year.

At the meetings of the Executive Committee, five persons shall constitute a quorum. A special meeting of the Executive Committee shall be called by the President, on the written application of three of its members.

XXVII. All proposals for alteration of the By-Laws shall be presented to the Society in writing, and shall be referred, without debate, to a special Committee, who shall consider and report on the same at the next annual meeting of the Society.

FORM OF SUBSCRIPTION.

The subscribers agree to comply with the By-Laws of the Massachusetts Homœopathic Medical Society.

Massachusetts Homœopathic Medical Society.

The Semi-Annual Meeting will be held in the Meionaon Hall, Tremont Temple, Boston, on Wednesday, Oct. 12, 1864, at 10 o'clock A. M.

In the morning session, the following, among other papers will be read.

The Early History of Homœopathy in Massachusetts; *by* Samuel Gregg, M. D.

Various Operations for Cataract with Recent Modifications; *by* H. C. Angell, M. D.

On the Hypodermic Injection of Medicines Homœopathically Indicated; *by* J H. Woodbury, M. D.

Members are requested to prepare and present at this Session, papers on any Medical Subject.

A collation will be provided between 12 and 1.

In the afternoon session the subject of discussion will be Dysentery. As a *verbatim* report of the discussion will be entered on the records, members are requested to give, in a concise form their observations in regard to this disease the present season; its peculiar character and frequency, and the therapeutic action of any medicines with their distinctive indications.

Any clinical reports may be forwarded to the *Committee on Clinical Medicine*, S. M. Cate, M. D. of Salem. Attention is called to the importance of filling out the *Statistical Records* and forwarding them to Dr Cate at the close of the year.

Any "medical provings" may be forwarded to the Chairman of the Committee on *Materia Medica*, H. L. Chase, M. D. of Cambridge.

The following persons have been approved for membership by the Executive Committee.

For Honorary Members:

Constantine Herring, M.D. of Philadelphia; John F. Gray, M.D. of New York; F. F. Quinn, M.D. of London; G. H. G. Jahr, M.D. of Paris; J. Fleischmann, M.D. of Vienna.

For Corresponding Members:

Wm. E. Paine, M.D. of Bath, Me.; Alpheus Morrill, M.D. of Concord, N. H. A. Howard Okie, M.D. of Providence, R. I. Henry M. Paine, M.D. of Clinton, N. Y. Carroll Dunham, M.D. of New York City; C. Neidhard, M.D. of Philadelphia; Walter Williamson, M. D. of Philadelphia; J. H. Pulte, M.D. of Cincinnati, O. R. Ludlam, M.D. of Chicago, Ill. Wm. T. Helsmith, M.D. of St. Louis, Mo. Arthur Fisher, M.D. of Montreal, C.W.

The Censors and Executive Committee will hold sessions for the examination and approval of Candidates for membership.

I. T. TALBOT, Recording Sec'y.

Boston, Oct. 4, 1864.

www.ingramcontent.com/pod-product-compliance
Lightning Source LLC
LaVergne TN
LVHW010833120826
845149LV00016B/1356